EXTREME SPORTS
No Limits!

Extreme Mountain Biking

Kelley MacAulay & Bobbie Kalman

Crabtree Publishing Company

www.crabtreebooks.com

Created by Bobbie Kalman

Dedicated by Jeff Rees
To Julian and Sebastian, the next generation riders—respect mother nature and she will reward you!

Editor-in-Chief
Bobbie Kalman

Writing team
Kelley MacAulay
Bobbie Kalman

Substantive editor
Kathryn Smithyman

Editors
Molly Aloian
Robin Johnson
Rebecca Sjonger

Design
Katherine Kantor

Production coordinator
Heather Fitzpatrick

Photo research
Crystal Foxton

Consultants
Pete Webber, Communications Director,
International Mountain Bicycling Association

Joe Breeze, Charter Member,
Mountain Bike Hall of Fame, Crested Butte, Colorado
http://www.mtnbikehalloffame.com

Special thanks to
Paul Philp, Sue Philp, and World Wide Cycle Supply

Illustrations
Bonna Rouse: pages 10, 11

Photographs
John Gibson: front cover, title page, pages 4, 12, 13, 14, 15,
    16, 17, 20, 21, 22, 23, 24, 25, 26, 27, 29, 30
Vincent Curutchet/DPPI/Icon SMI: page 28
Sterling Lorence: page 19
Peter Krutzik/PK Photography: page 18
© Wende Cragg, Rolling Dinosaur Archives: pages 6, 7
World Wide Cycle Supply: pages 8, 9
Other images by Digital Vision

Crabtree Publishing Company

www.crabtreebooks.com   1-800-387-7650

Cataloging-in-Publication Data
MacAulay, Kelley.
  Extreme mountain biking / Kelley MacAulay & Bobbie Kalman.
    p. cm. -- (Extreme sports no limits!)
  Includes index.
  ISBN-13: 978-0-7787-1678-5 (rlb)
  ISBN-10: 0-7787-1678-3 (rlb)
  ISBN-13: 978-0-7787-1724-9 (pbk)
  ISBN-10: 0-7787-1724-0 (pbk)
  1. All terrain cycling--Juvenile literature. 2. Extreme sports--Juvenile literature.
I. Kalman, Bobbie. II. Title. III. Series.
  GV1056.M28 2006
  796.63--dc22
                                            2005035787
                                            LC

**Published in
the United States**

PMB16A
350 Fifth Ave.
Suite 3308
New York, NY
10118

**Published
in Canada**

616 Welland Ave.
St. Catharines, Ontario
Canada
L2M 5V6

**Published in the
United Kingdom**

White Cross Mills
High Town, Lancaster
LA1 4XS
United Kingdom

**Published
in Australia**

386 Mt. Alexander Rd.
Ascot Vale (Melbourne)
VIC 3032

CONTENTS

Extreme Mountain Biking

Mountain biking is an **extreme sport**. Extreme sports are daring, high-speed competitions in which athletes showcase incredible tricks. In mountain biking, people ride mountain bikes over different types of **terrain**. Terrain is a natural area of land, such as a rocky mountainside.

Pro Bikers

Professional or "pro" mountain bikers earn a living by riding mountain bikes. They are **sponsored** by companies that make mountain bikes and equipment. Pro mountain bikers also win money at mountain-biking competitions.

THE NEED FOR SPEED

Mountain biking has many **disciplines**, or styles. Some disciplines are races. In **downhill races**, athletes race down steep mountainsides. **Cross-country** or **"XC" races** can last several hours as riders bike through **courses**. XC courses include challenging uphill and downhill sections of land. The longest mountain-biking races are **endurance races**—they can last over a week! In **hillclimb races**, riders race up steep mountains. In **dual-slalom** and **mountain-cross races**, riders race head-to-head on courses that include jumps and sharp turns.

ANYTHING GOES

Some disciplines of mountain biking focus on techniques and tricks, rather than on speed. **Observed trials** test a rider's balance as he or she moves through an **obstacle**-filled course. In **dirt jumping**, riders launch themselves off jumps made of dirt and perform tricks in the air. **Freeride competitions** test a rider's ability to perform tricks. A freerider must be able to handle a bike on any terrain, including **cliff-drops**, jumps, and natural obstacles such as logs.

EXTREME DANGER!

Extreme mountain biking requires incredible skill and balance. The riders shown in this book are professionals who trained for years to race and perform tricks on their bikes. Do not attempt anything shown in this book!

5

TAKIN' IT TO THE MOUNTAINS

Some riders added gears to their clunkers to make them easier to pedal up hills.

Before the 1970s, most cyclists used **road bikes** on paved roads. Road bikes have **gears**, which riders can shift to make riding on steep terrain easier. Riding road bikes **off-road**, or off paved roads, was not practical, however. The bikes had light, delicate frames and thin, smooth tires that would not grip uneven surfaces. Some people rode **BMX bikes**, which were invented in the 1960s. BMX bikes had sturdy frames and wide tires, but they did not have gears or large wheels, so they were also difficult to ride on hilly terrain.

MAKING IT WORK

In the 1970s, some riders in California started riding older bikes off-road. These old bikes were made between the 1930s and 1950s and were called **clunkers**. Clunkers had stronger frames and fatter tires than did road bikes. The large wheels of clunkers rolled easily over rough surfaces. Their knobby tires were covered in big bumps called **lugs**, which gave riders more **traction**, or grip on the ground. In 1977, the first bike designed specifically for off-road use was invented.

LET THE RACES BEGIN!

In 1976, clunker riders began testing their skills against one another in downhill and XC races. In 1983, a group of riders formed the National Off-Road Bicycle Association (NORBA). NORBA established rules for the races and organized official competitions.

GAINING POPULARITY

By the early 1980s, the easy-to-ride mountain bike was attracting many new people to the sport. It wasn't long before bicycle companies all over North America began making mountain bikes. By the late 1980s, mountain bikes were outselling all other styles of bikes! Throughout the 1990s, bicycle companies continued to improve the design of mountain bikes. They added **suspension** (see page 8) and made the frames lighter and stronger. They also added **indexed gears,** which made it easier for riders to shift gears.

TIMELINE

1976-1979: *Joe Breeze, shown below with his all-new mountain bike in 1977, wins ten of Marin County's 24 Repack downhills, which were the first off-road races.*

1979: *Gary Fisher and Charlie Kelly form Mountain Bikes, the first bicycle company to specialize in making mountain bikes.*

1983: *NORBA forms and organizes the first official competitions for mountain bikers.*

1988: *The International Mountain Bicycling Association (IMBA) is formed to help create and protect safe trails for riders.*

1990: *The Union Cycliste Internationale (UCI) organizes the first Mountain Bike World Championships.*

1991: *The UCI organizes the first Mountain Biking World Cup competition.*

1996: *Mountain-biking events are added to the Summer Olympics.*

THE BIKES

In the last 30 years, **mountain-bike technology** has improved by leaps and bounds. Bike frames are lighter and stronger than they once were. Most mountain bikes also have knobby tires and suspension. Suspension is like a big metal spring. During hard landings, the suspension spring **contracts** and absorbs much of the impact.

rear suspension

front suspension

DOWNHILL BIKE

*Riders in many disciplines, including downhill, observed trials, dirt jump, dual slalom, and freeride, use **platform**, or flat, pedals. These pedals allow the riders to **dab**, or touch their feet to the ground quickly.*

FRAMED!

Different disciplines of mountain biking require different bikes. Most bikes have **titanium** or **aluminum** frames. Both of these metals are strong and lightweight, but titanium is the stronger and more expensive metal. Bikes designed for some races have stronger frames than those designed for other races. For example, downhill bikes have bigger, heavier frames than do XC bikes. The big, strong frames of downhill bikes can handle rough rides on **treacherous** terrain. The lightweight frames of XC bikes are better for riding long distances and making sudden **sprints**.

XC BIKE

Most mountain bikes have between 21 and 27 gears. Having many gears allows riders to tackle incredibly steep hills.

*XC, hillclimb, and endurance riders often choose **clipless pedals**. Clipless pedals have small clips that hook into the rider's shoes. The clips help prevent the rider's feet from slipping off the pedals.*

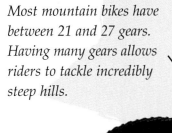

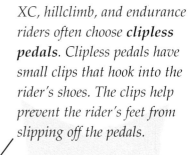

SUSPENSION

Mountain bikes can be **full suspension**, **hardtail**, or **rigid**. Full-suspension bikes have front and rear suspension. Hardtail bikes have only front suspension. Rigid bikes have no suspension. Suspension makes bikes heavier, so riders may use hardtail or rigid bikes for competitions in which they need to move quickly or perform tricks in the air. For example, XC riders or dirt jumpers sometimes use hardtail or rigid bikes.

Suspension technology has come a long way, however, and it is now lighter than ever. Today, many riders in each discipline choose to ride full-suspension bikes for better control.

TIRES

Different mountain bikes have different types of tires. XC bikes usually have lightweight tires. Downhill bikes have huge tires with large lugs. Bikes for observed trials have fat, soft tires that grip obstacles.

SAFETY CHECK

Extreme mountain bikers perform incredible stunts and ride at high speeds, so they need to wear equipment that protects their bodies. Riders choose protective equipment that is comfortable and allows them to move freely.

*Downhill, freeride, and dirt-jump riders are at risk of getting injured during **wipeouts**, or falls. These riders wear **full-face helmets**. Full-face helmets have shields that cover riders' faces.*

*Riders wear goggles under their helmets to protect their eyes from **debris** such as dirt and objects such as tree branches.*

*Riders who use platform pedals wear flexible shoes that have deep treads. Shoes with deep treads grip the pedals' **pins**.*

*Downhill, freeride, and dirt-jump riders wear **body armor** while riding. Body armor is protective equipment made of hard plastic. These riders also wear guards that cover their elbows, knees, and shins.*

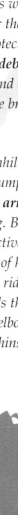

XC, hillclimb, and endurance riders usually wear **open-face helmets**. These helmets do not cover the riders' faces.

XC riders wear tight clothing made of **spandex**. Many riders wear shorts that have padded inserts on which the riders sit. The inserts keep riders comfortable during the many hours they spend on their bikes.

Riders often wear gloves to protect their hands during wipeouts.

Riders who use clipless pedals wear shoes that have **cleats** on the bottoms. The cleats lock onto the pedals. Riders twist their feet to the side to release their shoes from the pedals.

clipless pedal

11

THE LOWDOWN ON DOWNHILL

Downhill racing is one of the most popular disciplines of mountain biking. In competitions, athletes race one by one down steep mountain trails that have bumps, jumps, and **berms**, or banked curves. Most of the trails are a half-mile to three-miles (0.8-4.8 km) long and have loose surfaces.

SPEED DEMONS

Downhill riders charge down slopes at speeds of up to 60 miles per hour (96.5 kph)! As they race downhill, the riders pedal to continue increasing their speeds. Some riders travel so fast, that they can complete a course that is two miles (3.2 km) long in less than five minutes! The rider who crosses the finish line with the fastest time wins the race.

*Every downhill course is different. **Course designers**, or people who create courses, make sure every course has different obstacles and challenges.*

TECHNICAL DIFFICULTIES

Racing downhill may sound easy, but downhill racing actually requires incredible bike-handling abilities. Downhill racers can ride over logs, rocks, roots, and cliff-drops without wiping out. One minute the racers are flying straight downhill, and the next minute they must slam on their brakes in order to ride over logs or rocks. Riders must be able to maneuver around turns and obstacles without losing control of their bikes. They have to be ready for anything!

EXTREME XC

XC racing is one of the best-known disciplines of mountain biking. XC was the first discipline to become an Olympic event. XC racers ride many laps around a course that is four-to-six miles (6.4-9.6 km) long. Most courses have difficult terrain and obstacles such as tree roots, rocks, and streams that cut across the trails. Riders must compete nonstop for hours, while still maintaining the necessary strength to take off into sprints when they near the finish line. The first person to cross the finish line wins the race.

A CLASS ACT

XC competitors are divided into classes based on their abilities. Riders in different classes compete in races of different lengths. The beginner class rides for 18 to 22 miles (28.9-35.4 km). These riders are great athletes, but they compete only for fun. Pros make up the top class of riders. They race for about 30 miles (48.2 km) in each competition.

XC courses often have challenging uphill sections.

LEADER OF THE PACK

Riders in a **road race** begin a race slowly and pace themselves as they go. Riders in an XC race take off quickly right from the start of a race, however. Every racer wants to be at the head of the pack, so that he or she will not be held up by other racers along the way. As the race continues, the riders become separated from one another, based on their strength and abilities.

Riders are not allowed much help during their rides. If their tires blow out or their equipment breaks, the riders must fix the problem themselves. People on the sidelines provide riders with food and drinks, however. The food and drinks keep riders going during XC competitions that last for hours.

EPIC ENDURANCE

Endurance races are the longest competitions in mountain biking. Although every rider wants to win, many endurance competitors are satisfied just to reach the finish line! Endurance competitions can last for six to eight hours, although many last for 24 hours. Some competitions can even last a whole week! Endurance riders either make one lap on an extremely long course, or they make multiple laps on a shorter course.

DAY-LONG ENDURANCE

Many endurance races that are 24 hours long have two categories: team and solo. In the team category, riders compete in teams made up of four or five people. The members of the team compete one at a time, allowing the other team members time to rest. The riders on each team decide how often each rider will hit the trail. In the solo category, each racer must complete the entire race on his or her own!

Endurance courses present riders with many challenges, including uphill sections, obstacles, and long, winding sections that may run through forests.

ICY IDITABIKE

One of the most challenging endurance races is the Iditabike, which takes place in February each year. The race is a journey through 100 miles (160 km) of Alaskan wilderness. Riders travel through dark forests, over slippery hills, and even across frozen lakes and rivers!

Riders have 50 hours to complete the course. An even longer race than the Iditabike is the Iditabike Extreme. This race takes place on a grueling course that is 320 miles (515 km) long. The course winds through an Alaskan mountain range. The race takes riders about one week to complete!

For many riders, one of the most appealing aspects of endurance races is the challenge of riding through rough terrain at night. Riders have only small lights on their bikes and helmets to help them see in the dark.

UP TO THE CHALLENGE

In a hillclimb competition, riders begin at the bottom of a long, steep slope and race up the slope to the finish line. The course often stretches uphill for miles! In some hillclimb competitions, riders race through the course one at a time. Other competitions begin with a **mass start**, in which all riders race at the same time.

CLIMBING TO THE TOP

Riding uphill is not the only challenge hillclimb racers face. The courses also have obstacles around which the riders must maneuver successfully, without allowing one of their competitors to take the lead! The racer who crosses the finish line in the shortest time wins the race.

*Hillclimb competitors must train for years to increase their strength and **stamina**. Stamina is the ability to continue an activity, even when the activity is very difficult.*

Hillclimb competitions test each rider's level of fitness and dedication to the sport.

HEATED BATTLES

Many mountain-biking competitions take place on courses that are spread out over long distances. Spectators at these events often get to see only a few moments of the action as the athletes speed past on their bikes. Dual slalom and mountain cross are exciting competitions that take place on small, but challenging, courses. The smaller courses allow spectators to watch entire races. Each course has many bumps, jumps, **whoops**, and berms. The most difficult aspect of dual slalom and mountain cross, however, is the intense competition. The riders cannot allow themselves to be intimidated by the other riders just behind them, who are always trying to steal the lead position.

Many courses for dual slalom and mountain cross are marked with flags, around which riders must twist and turn without falling.

To win in mountain cross, athletes must be very aggressive, powerful riders. Brian Lopes is the hottest star in mountain cross. Read more about him on page 28.

ONE-ON-ONE

In dual slalom, two riders compete against each other in separate lanes. The riders begin side-by-side at the starting gate and take off when the gate drops open. Although organizers try to make both lanes the same, sometimes one is better than the other. After racing each other, the riders switch lanes and race again. The rider with the best combined time is the winner.

LEADER OF THE PACK

In mountain cross, four to six riders compete at the same time. The first rider out of the starting gate has a huge advantage over the other riders, although this rider will not always win the race. A skilled racer can quickly **strategize**, or plan, to choose the best path around the course. With so many riders on the course, wipeouts occur often. Riders must be skilled at handling their bikes in order to cope with the challenges of the course and to avoid riders who fall across their paths.

BIKERS ON TRIAL

In observed trials, riders hop and jump their bikes around obstacle courses. The obstacles include large rocks, metal rails, huge logs, steep cliff-drops, and basically anything else the course designers can think of! Riders have to complete the courses without putting down one of their feet or falling. They are given points every time they fall or dab. At the end of the competition, the rider with the fewest points wins.

*Bikes used for observed trials have extra-tough back wheels because the riders often use their back wheels to hop onto obstacles or over **gaps**.*

FOR THE FUN OF IT

Some observed-trials riders do not enter competitions. Instead, these riders take to the hills and tackle every natural obstacle they come across. Just for fun, they fly across huge gaps, jump off cliffs, and ride to the top of the biggest obstacles they can find. Many observed-trials riders who live in cities practice their sport in **terrain parks**. A terrain park is an area that has many obstacles on which extreme athletes can ride.

AIRBORNE ATHLETES

Dirt jumping is a style of mountain biking that is all about **getting air**, or flying up into the air. Dirt jumpers perform on a course that is made up of a series of jumps. The jumps are mounds of packed dirt that have steep, sloping sides. Riders take off from the jumps and fly into the air. They get as much air as possible to give themselves time to perform tricks. The riders who impress the judges by performing the best tricks win the competitions.

CAN-CAN

To perform a **can-can**, shown above, a rider swings one leg over the bike, so that both legs are on the same side.

Dirt jumpers must control their fear in order to perform tricks with style and perfect technique.

NO-FOOTER

To perform a **no-footer**, a rider lifts himself or herself off the bike seat and kicks both legs out to the side, away from the pedals.

SPINS

Riders perform spins by turning around on their bikes in the air. Spins are named for the number of times a rider rotates in the air. For example, a full turn is called a **360** because the rider rotates 360° in the air.

FLIPS

To perform a flip such as this one, a rider flies off a jump and then turns head over heels in midair. Riders practice flips on trampolines to learn how to regain their landing positions before reaching the ground.

25

FREERIDE

Freeride mountain biking is for adventurous riders who want to go anywhere and do anything on their mountain bikes! Freeriding is influenced by other mountain-biking disciplines. It involves the extreme speeds of downhill racing, the obstacles of observed trials, and the challenging tricks of dirt jumping.

THRILL-SEEKERS

Freeriders always want to make their rides more challenging. They seek out the most extreme terrain nature has to offer. If nature is not extreme enough, however, freeriders often create their own obstacles! They build narrow rails and bridges, pile up huge logs, and construct seesaws to make natural areas that are similar to terrain parks.

To freeriders, no obstacle is off-limits. They will attempt to ride up cliffs, along walls, or over deep gaps.

This freerider is taking on a narrow, winding bridge high above the forest floor.

COMPETITIONS

Although many freeriders ride only for fun, some take part in competitions. Freeride competitions are thrilling shows for spectators! The courses are set in natural areas, where the terrain offers opportunities for tricks such as **wall-rides**, cliff-drops, and gap jumps. To impress the judges, riders perform as many jaw-dropping stunts as they can. They are often judged on the difficulty and style of their performances, as well as for their bike-handling abilities.

MOUNTAIN BIKING STARS

Pro mountain bikers are incredible athletes who are dedicated to advancing their sport. Some of the stars on these pages are legends of the sport who set the standards for today's athletes. Others are newcomers who are working to take mountain biking to new heights. After years of training, these stars are some of the best athletes in the world.

BRIAN LOPES

Nobody rides mountain cross like American star Brian Lopes. Like many other mountain-biking champions, Lopes got his start riding BMX bikes. After racing BMX bikes for eleven years, Lopes was ready to take on a new challenge. He tried out mountain biking and was soon winning competitions. Lopes has won the World Championship and World Cup titles. He has also won more mountain-cross races than any other rider in the world.

ANNE-CAROLINE CHAUSSON

French rider Anne-Caroline Chausson, shown right, is an incredible downhill mountain-bike racer. Although she got her start as a BMX World Champion, Chausson had no trouble conquering the world of mountain biking. Chausson has won more downhill and mountain cross World Cup and World Championship titles than any other female rider. In fact, she won the World Championship title fifteen times in a row! Chausson has also set a downhill speed record of 117 miles per hour (188.3 kph) while riding a rigid bike! She is an inspiration to both female and male riders.

PAULA PEZZO

Italian rider Paula Pezzo is one of the best cross-country mountain bikers in the world. Not only has she won the World Cup and World Championship titles, she is also the only person to have won two Olympic medals in mountain biking. Pezzo won gold at the 1996 and 2000 Olympics in women's cross-country racing.

NICOLAS VOUILLOZ

Retired rider Nicolas Vouilloz is one of the greatest riders to compete in downhill racing. After growing up riding BMX bikes and motorcycles around the hills of France, Vouilloz was prepared to take on the world of downhill mountain biking. He won an amazing ten World Championships. His competitors felt that Vouilloz's skills were so great that they nicknamed him "the Alien!" Today, Vouilloz is passing on his skills to members of the downhill racing team he owns.

DARREN BERRECLOTH

After getting his start in freestyle BMX, Canadian rider Darren "Bearclaw" Berrecloth, shown above, made a move to freeride mountain biking and changed the sport forever. Berrecloth won competition after competition by being the first person to perform BMX tricks in freeride mountain-biking competitions. Although he is only in his early twenties, Berrecloth is sure to become a legend of his sport.

JUMP ON IN

Mountain biking isn't only about extreme tricks and competitions. It's a great sport for people of all ages. Riders can hit the trails in their areas to stay fit and healthy, and also have a great time! If you feel tempted to try out some of the amazing moves of the pros, keep in mind that they have trained for years to be at the top of their game. Many of the pros have also been injured many times as they mastered their sports. Keep reading to learn some important riding safety tips.

SAFE RIDING

Mountain biking is a lot of fun when riders are safe, but it can be a very dangerous sport if riders are careless or disrespectful of one another. Never ride a bike without wearing a helmet! You should also wear equipment, such as pads, to protect yourself against injuries during wipeouts.

Not sure where to ride this summer? Try your local ski resort! Many ski resorts across North America now allow mountain bikers to hit the slopes and trails in the summer months. You may even be able to use special lifts to get your bike up the mountains, as shown above.

TAKE IT FROM THOSE WHO KNOW

The International Mountain Bicycling Association is dedicated to creating and maintaining safe areas where mountain bikers can hit the trails and have fun. In order to enjoy this privilege, however, riders have to protect both themselves and the environment. Below are some tips from IMBA that will help you enjoy your ride, respect the environment, and keep the trails safe for the future.

- Never ride on closed trails—they are closed for a reason!
- Never travel off a trail, or scare or hurt animals.
- Put a bell on your bike to warn other riders that you are coming down the trail.
- Slow down when you are approaching other trail-users and pass them carefully.
- Never leave trash behind on the trail. If you see trash, pick it up and put it in a garbage can.

GLOSSARY

Note: Boldfaced words that are defined in the text may not appear in the glossary.

cliff-drop A trick in which a biker rides his or her bike off a cliff and lands on the ground below

contract To become smaller in size

course A section of land that is used or designed for mountain-biking competitions

debris Small pieces of rock and dirt that fly into the air as a mountain biker rides

gap A wide space between two cliffs or objects over which riders jump

indexed gear A type of gear that allows a rider to move a lever or twist a handle grip to cause the bike to change automatically from one gear to another

mountain-bike technology Scientific knowledge used to make mountain bikes

obstacle An object on which mountain bikers perform tricks

pin A small spike on a bike pedal

road race A cross-country race in which athletes perform on a paved surface

spandex A stretchy fabric made from synthetic materials

sponsor To pay an athlete money to wear a company's clothing or to use its equipment

sprint To ride at top speed for a short period of time

treacherous Describing steep, dangerous terrain

wall ride A trick in which a biker rides his or her mountain bike up a wall

whoops Sets of rounded bumps found on a dual-slalom or mountain-cross course

INDEX

1 2 3 4 5 6 7 8 9 0   Printed in the U.S.A.   5 4 3 2 1 0 9 8 7 6